AM1

AMNION

Stephanie Sy-Quia

GRANTA

Granta Trust, 12 Addison Avenue, London W11 4QR

First published in Great Britain by Granta Poetry, 2021

Copyright © Stephanie Sy-Quia, 2021

Stephanie Sy-Quia has asserted her moral right under the Copyright,
Designs and Patents Act, 1988, to be identified as the author of this work.

The acknowledgements on pages 111–12 constitute an extension
of this copyright page.

The photograph on page 109 is from the author's private collection.

A CIP catalogue record for this book is available from the British Library.

1 3 5 7 9 10 8 6 4 2

ISBN 978 1 78378 774 6
eISBN 978 1 78378 826 2

Typeset in Minion by Hamish Ironside

Printed and bound in Great Britain by TJ Books, Padstow

ⲀⲚⲞⲔ ⲠⲈ ⲠϢⲀϪⲈ Ⲙ̄ ⲠⲀⲢⲀⲚ·

I am the utterance of my name

CONTENTS

Part I: Spandrels

spandrel (church): shoulders, in part, an arch.
spandrel (biology): that which has not arisen from fear.

My parents collided on opposing bicycles outside the Radcliffe Camera.
They were married on a grey Westminster morning.
They ate grapes afterwards.

I remember my first encounter with a cathedral: the Parvis de Notre-
Dame in the rain. I was a small pink anorak. I was looking at a skyscraper
studded with kings. Unfathomable to me that a skyscraper could be so
old.

(A fathom is the distance between outstretched hands)

My father was born on an island brushed by the hem of the monsoon.

My mother was born on the Sahara's edge:
blonde, with blue eyes in the dark hands
of the doctor
who slapped her
to breath.

In the beginning, the begetting. Leda, Mary, Igraine, the Sabines, the
mothers of Theseus and Heracles: blessed among women.

One of this story's beginnings takes place in my grandmother's nineteen-year-old body. This was a body into which the catechism had been carved so as to keep it blank. She knew nothing of men and their urges. We think.

room 10a of the British Museum: considered the sport of kings,

My grandmother was nineteen when she went down on her back
not
knowing why –
the islands,
her hacienda on a hill,
and her pearls from the boy
who later gave her
two black eyes.

They tell me you would have married pink
to have a cook bring you rice, sticky in banana leaves;
had you not moved wetly
with the black-pearl boy who didn't
really want you.

Two black eyes
held wet and shining
in the palms of the hands –

so you were sent away –
and came back with two black eyes
and a baby boy.

I was a crop of dark curls skinned soft with love. I was cramming my
pockets with sea glass until my yellow mac sagged. There was my mother,
splintering the sun with her head, and there was my father walking silent
on the sand.

My parents, panathenaic in the light of redwoods: so strong and beautiful,
and so young – how the ocean roared behind my mother freezing in a
frame – I remember an ocean the colour of an eye –

> Colossal marble statue of a recumbent lion; carved with
> inlaid eyes, originally probably of glass, now missing.

> The Lion of Knidos's empty sockets would have held eyes of
> glass
> to help ships off Halikarnassus.
> Weighing twelve tons,
> it sits ironic in the inky heart
> of London

> an emblem of empire,

blind.

When the Wall fell my mother was twenty-one and she cried because this was the end of the world as she had known it.

In the place where I grew up there were horses,
thighs moving like nudity under their fur.
The pigeons are clattering into the heights now

> (in the British Museum there are shards of horse)
> (in the British Museum there is a blind lion)

My grandfather collected lions.

Empires are like milk teeth.
They fall.

It is only in European epistemologies that the desert (or the jungle, or the dragon bay) is configured as a void, and therefore, the backdrop for the single blanching passion, as per *Moon Tiger*, *Out of Africa*, *Indochine*.
And of my mother's birth, and the doctor's darker hands? Why did I make mention?
These are the tropes that gape.

Fleeing the High Gothic.

When my father got tuberculosis they drained the water from his lungs so he wouldn't drown inside himself.

The water had been rising in him for twenty-one years,
in and out of pale love and a stepfather.

I saw the stepfather once: he was creased and putting French fries in his mouth.
My father steered us away with hands on our backs.

My parents married, and afterwards ate grapes.

The Home Office posted someone to their corner, to watch that in their goings out and in their comings in they were together, and at nights.

Of my parents' early loving, I rightfully know little.

My grandmother Lola liked to go to parties. She was the favourite child
of wealthy landowners. They lived in a hacienda on a hill overlooking
Manila. They had twenty-five servants and hardwood floors. Her father
had fifty horses. She had a pair of shoes to match every dress, with gloves
and bags besides. I know, because she tells me.

My father was born because the boy gave her pearls
and gave her black eyes and the pearls scatter-bounced over the balayong
parquet

       (shall I entertain you with the fetishism of a foreign name?)
because she had not known

             of his scales.

There was no grandeur in what we suspect was New Year's Eve 1965.
He was Spanish new money; unsuitable. Lola was the most beautiful
debutante in Manila. Appropriated Chinese firecrackers whistled outside
and the party murmured below.

They were married by a Jesuit (always an emphatic detail).
They slunk off from the movies for an afternoon
and gave their chaperone (her brother) the slip.
For this, her mother hit her round the face

         with a shoe.

To run with a baby: a primal thing. On such flights are founded myths,
and cities. Jochebed, Danae, Florence Owens Thompson. These are the
mothers whose names we do not need to know.

After the black eyes: to Munich, where a friend could hide her. (If the location seems improbable, no matter.)
And he chased her.

In the hall one night the lobster-black lacquer-clad telephone rang, or maybe it was a yellow ticker-taped telegram, saying
Get out of Munich!
So further south, to Vienna.
She was enrolled in secretarial school and it was agreed like the handover of a sometime protectorate that her son, my father, would go back to Manila.
He would stay in the hacienda on the hill with his grandmother, who rang for mangoes with a tiny silver bell.
He would have a little nipa hut to play in.
And a toy car bought specially in Hong Kong, for him to skid round corners of the hardwood-floored house, with the big awnings and the sliding capiz panes.
He would be rescued in a typhoon by the gardener, who gave him a piggyback through the flood.

Meanwhile, my grandmother Lola learned to touch-type,
read the tempers of the monied and entertain their wives.
Her sometime husband desisted.   ·
        (There was an annulment, divorce being non grata in that country.)
            (Ordained by bribe, with my father, the evidence, hidden away.)
She had strict instructions to get a new one.
She met an Austrian steel salesman. When my father was five she came to fetch him back, for Spain. And he did not know who she was.

If we are to go back again: there were three sisters (great-great-aunts) by
names of Fe, Esperanza and Caridad.

In the underdiscussed Massacre of Manila (February 1945),
Fe was widowed in the two-for-one, street-by-street Japanese retreat.
At the creak of bootstep on the stair
she bassinet-snatched her sleeping baby,
and hid in a cupboard.
Sure enough in comes a soldier and from the cupboard-crack Fe can see
he bassinet-bayonets immediately.

Esperanza became a vegan and a nun.
Now she mothers superior and Carmelite near Loag

> (shall I entertain you with the fetishism of a foreign name?)
my father when a little boy was taken to the visiting room which is
latticed-split and asked

> 'are you a bird?

> > because

> > > you are

> > > > in a cage.'

Caridad was five years wed, and childless: an enigma to all invested.
She sustained dumdum fire in the same-said Japanese retreat –
caught in crossfire on the walk home from consoling the women of her
family

> > (brother, father: men all rounded up)
> > (a soldier, sniper-slain, and a radius drawn where he fell
> > > from which to take all the men to be found)
Caridad's husband, gesturing from a first-floor window for her to stop

but she misread him, and he jumped as she fell in the street, a bullet
expanding in her back.

Luckily her neighbour was an obstetrician and stitched her up facedown
between the stirrups,
having only whiskey to clean what would become a fist-fit hollow in her
back.
He had time to see her uterus was retrograde so he rectified,
and Lola was born in March of 1946.

Back again, elsewhere: my other grandmother was born in Sheffield in
1927. Her mother was a red-headed singer with a rare name. Her father
was a man who made reservoirs. Splinting to support the necks of valleys,
dismantling country houses to loose floods upon them. On the last day
before the disappearance of Derwent House, he went in and it was almost
bare, with only floorboards wide as cows made of seventeenth-century
oak. So he ripped those up too, and made a coffee table. On drought days
you can still see mud prints of the great house. Sheffield being a place up
in arms in years of *the war*, Nana's homework was blared open each night
between the ages of twelve and eighteen. Her father the engineer, who was
thought of as more value, slotted his car into the tracks of trams so as to
drive in the dark for a deeper safety, his wife and child led to shallower
shelter. She went to Oxford in 1945. Her village pooled cloth rations so
she could have a suit. She lived off crumpets with no butter. She lost her
Riding accent to the rounded vowels of the south. In that gold and spired
city, she dreamed that all the cyclists in their gowns turned to crows and
lifted off the cobbled road; that she woke in the closed part of an upper E
for an exam. She refers, offhand, to boyfriends in this period, and smoking
cigarettes, going to visit one (a stained-glass craftsman, she loved to watch
him work) in the Great Smog.

At twenty-six her parents died within six weeks of one another (a heart attack, a broken heart). She became a Catholic and went to Rome to study theology. She lived in a new build on a hill behind the Vatican. Perhaps she tried to become a nun. She wrote a book on Julian of Norwich and how God is actually the mother.

She falls awkwardly into the binaries. She was not the fleeing pin-up girl that begins most bildungsromane. She was not the smooth-skinned vahine that I have just described for you in Lola, my other grandmother. Instead, she wanted a retranslation of the Gospel of Matthew, because the word used of Jesus's mother in the Old Hebrew Bible is *almah*, meaning only 'young woman', and the Greek Septuagint describes her as *parthenos*,

       young holy woman

          with the *implication* of

              virgin.

She wanted to sweep aside millennia worth of staggered mistranslations – she was a woman who believed that a great deal of harm had been done by peritexts.

One of this story's beginnings takes place in my grandmother's forty-year-old body, which was rare at the time.

  ⁂

They met in Rome. He was a priest. They must have fucked
because he was *defrocked.*

The angelus. The houses the colours of gelato.
It was at the time of the Second Vatican Council.
God could be in English.
No one had prepared them for this rupture.

They married and fled to Libya
and my grandmother cut up her winter coat to make a teddy bear
(being pregnant).

(When he was dying, his Latin passed out of him like a spell,
and he wept like one bereaved. Nana held his hand
and rummaged in the husks of it.)

(It is Angela Carter who writes in *The Sadeian Woman*
that an irony of the missionary position being so
enshrined by a misogynistic church is that
the man must approach the woman on his knees.)

He was cast out from its great frame.
  – did he still pray?
  – I don't think anyone can say whether or not someone else is praying.

My Nana is in labour, but the road to the hospital in Misrata is some
200km from the village where my grandparents live: the road is rough
and constantly being reclaimed by sand, and my grandfather is driving
carefully. She is in labour for a long time, and the hospital does not have
pain medication. When the baby is born, it does not breathe. The doctor
swings it by the ankles and finally it sneezes.

My grandfather and my grandmother drive home, and all the while my
grandmother has the baby on her lap. As the sun rises, she shields my
mother from it with her hands. Her baby is the length of her hands.

When my father was living under-loved in Spain,
Caridad sent for him to come back to Manila,
Ensure he was fed mangoes and adobo.
    (He has talked about it very little. Except he would buy mangoes, impale
                        the stones on knives and give them to us to gnaw on.)
Caridad died of lung cancer on New Year's Eve 1985, before she could see
the revolution in her country. When it came, less than two months later,
my father was a student in the faraway half-hued country.
He finally cried an anniversary later. My mother had found him by then,
and was horrified to hear that he had hitherto spent Christmases walking
the streets of Barcelona by night (while his mother and brother and the
Austrian ate goose and stollen) (he did this by choice, so as to avoid the
Austrian). So she said:
        – Come stay with me.

During the Six-Day War they had to stockpile water and juice so that
my grandmother could still breastfeed.
They left just as Gaddafi was rising to power and went to West Germany.
Only an hour from the fence.
Guards and dogs and dummies with guns.

While they lived there they heard a story of two families in the East
who stockpiled synthetic clothing to make a hot air balloon. Stitched
up in a cellar: this wild, arlequin hope. It was inflated in the forest and
untethered, so they went there and then, no test run. All eight of them in
the little basket, skimming over the death strip with the Rottweilers and
razorwire and falling into the West with a broken arm or two between
them. Today you can see their hope hung out in the Museum of Escapes
or Mauermuseum in Berlin. It is so small and when she saw it, twenty
years after the Wall's fall, my mother cried.

My grandfather was born in Staffordshire. At eight he went to a boarding school where they had to crack the ice in the washbasins. At eighteen he went to Oxford and was a boxing blue. At twenty he joined *the war* and became an aerial navigator in Burma. There Some Thing Happened (like the void event at the centre of a modernist novel, we do not know), like a Murder or a Trauma, so after the war: Rome. He became a priest. Once my mother found a letter he had written to his mother whilst very young at school. The letter said *Please send me more cake.*

I am told my English great-grandmother was from an Old Catholic family.
I am not sure what an Old Catholic is or means.
She was one of thirteen children.
From her my grandfather had a monk's bench dating from before the dissolution
                    (he angered at Nana for getting big pot plant rings on its top.)
Her husband died in Lourdes:
a heart attack in a dust-scuffing crowd of palm-pressers come to see
the Virgin of the Yellow Roses cure the amputees.
He is buried there.
His name was Edwin.
I could go, if I wanted, and see his headstone.
I could buy a Madonna nightlamp and burn an elbow made of wax, sold from row upon row of tubs sorted by afflicted body part,
for some as yet unknown friend who suffered, presumably, from a funnybone.

In a flat in Barcelona you can glimpse – in the manner of a Degas painting, so inspired by the advent of photography and the possibilities of splicing up frames for snapshots, giving you a sense of having glimpsed a thing illicit – a belt or some other easy moniker. Somewhere behind a closed door you know without eyeslice that there is a little boy rocking (this is my father).

I lied.

My mother and my father met at a ball. In black tie, with marquee tents and lights in the trees. The green quads and stone the colour of sun-enamoured dust.

Then in earnest it began
with a postcard from Zamboanga
to which my father has never been
        but still.

My mother says it hadn't really occurred to either of them to fall in love with each other. She says when she married him, on that Euston Road October morning with the Ancient Assyrian lions, she didn't know. She was twenty-one; she knew nothing.

He says he started to fall in love with her on their first date, when she wore a borrowed dress and pretended to speak Dutch.
She was trying to prove that Dutch is just German spoken sideways.

People definitely thought he was handsome, but exotic. Not boyfriend material. They wouldn't take him home to meet their parents.
My father, being written of in the student paper:
Noel Sy-Quia, the Filipino . . .
I went to the Union because they had great parties, my mother told me.
They spoke German to each other, and annoyed everyone.

His student visa ran out.

For reasons I can understand, Lola never got him adopted by the
Austrian.

So while she had a passport in that chic shade of maroon, her son sat in
Barcelona waiting to be deported. Back to the Philippines where little love
waited for him.

Then my mother phoned him, and as I imagine in a manner she still
possesses today, she said:

> – Well I'll marry you then.

The blessing went like this:
Nana called my mother into her room,
where she was doing her hair
(at this time long, blonde with strong bars of ash)
piling it up with many pins
and said to my mother in the mirror

> – Are you sure?

                    and that was it.

       I think of the knuckles in low relief
       in Room 10a

my shoulders came forth softly furred in brown
neither did they know of the couching wings
folded in the space between my lungs

                   (The wings dark and leathery, their beat
                            intermittent but near-deadly)

my mother says

           it rises in you like a roar.

My father cried. In secret they counted all my toes. He took a picture of
me curled by a melon, because it amused him.

England was unknown to me then.
Consequently, my English is unrooted.

I turn these soft sounds over in my mouth, my throat, my jaw, when I am
walking or on my bike or peeling an onion. Island. English. Testing where
they fall, like knuckles.
Language of engels and angles and angels,
standing still while fastened to a stage-set of stippled gold, with their
wingtips dipped in peroxide and their tightly coiled curls.

This my gallery of kings.
One grandfather: Edward Lear and Rudyard Kipling, a life lacking in
women, boarding school, air force, Burma, Rome,
an adored only daughter.

The other grandfather is by and large a gap.

Burma is now Myanmar.

In the most immediate days upon Franco's disquisition-end,
my father then aged nine remembers
the Catalan flags which spilled from every balcony and window ledge,
quiet and defiant.

Though my name goes back and back through men
there was a flipping when my father had been born a year.
On his birth certificate he is named after his father, Antonio Trillio III
but pto and you will find a final uncoupling from this boy who beat my
grandmother.

For she overrode this name with her own; he is Noel Sy-Quia and so my name means to me that she put it into law that he was hers and would grow into the shape of this. So too have I and learned to love spelling it out loud and I will never give it up, this blip of matrilineality in too long a line of pater nosters.

Val de Grâce, St Michel in May, its great baroque-crusted dome vaulting like quintessential cakes sold at the Place de la Madeleine.
The groom is the son of Stéphanie,

she opens her arms wide to my father
Je te présente she says to a friend
le fils de ma très chère amie
il venait souvent passer les vacances avec moi
here she skates over why
alors tu vois, je n'ai aucune responsabilité biologique mais –

My parents collided in that gold and fevered city.

When she first met my mother, Lola was not yet forty. They went to a Chinese restaurant and she did nothing but speak Spanish to her son, and the only thing she said to my mother was

– Shall we get you a fork?
Later, when my father told Lola he was going to marry my mother, she asked

– Who?

'So what brings you here today?' (the young man who will become, among other things, my father) is in a cab now. They have pulled up outside Westminster Town Hall. He thinks. He has come far to be here, now: from the typhoons in Manila and his grandmother who loved him, and his mother with her Austrian husband, and the flat in Barcelona, and the boarding school in Yorkshire with its cold water and rugby stripes, and that girl on the bicycle – upon hearing his answer the cab driver laughs and does not charge him. He trips up the steps with the ring that he had forgotten to buy. And the young woman who would become, among other things, my mother: her hair is wisping like some woman on the big walls of the Tate as she stands on the steps flanked by the pseudo-Babylonian lions, wearing a white suit she made for work, and a white ribbon in her hair, holding an enormous bunch of roses, a detail of this ceremony which she too had forgotten until she got there and waiting at the steps was the mother of a friend in her tiny 2CV, rolling down the window for the roses – all five guests presumed my mother would forget flowers and so they brought some – and here he is, tripping up to her in his black suit, and here they all are in the pictures, everyone holding a bunch of flowers;

and now: the children who became my mother and my father are walking out into the cold light of dark-hearted London, flanked by lions, with gold circles on their fingers.

In the revolution
they hacked the bells from their beams
and weighing six tonnes
they crashed through their towers
to crack.

(We knew Huguenots, a many times great-grandfather of whom was
sent to row himself to death. His name on a memorial board high in the
Cévennes. Where people came running with their faith rolled up in their
arms; made flatpack pulpits to fold into barrels, made bibles so small
women could hide them in their hair. Those friends' daughter aged six
was asked on a history test

LOUIS XIV WAS
(A) A MONARCH
(B) A PRESIDENT
(C) A DICTATOR

When she circled c and her teacher gave a red no,
her father demanded a meeting, to say
              – to her he was a dictator)

Cluny was before Rome the biggest church in the Christian world, until
Napoleon ordered its debricking for a riding school. One side tower
remains, and large bronze medallions through the town mark out where
you would have been walking up the nave or near the font.

In that other city, you can see the footprint where the Wall used to be. And sometimes small signs: 1 Aug 1964, *zwei personen flücht*. I am interested in this *flücht*, which is flight, as in *to flee*, but also *to fly*. But they did not fly. They flung a carpet over the wire, and one broke an ankle. There is a rye field which will never be harvested, where the rusted wrought iron cross of a church which was blown up and blown open has been left, mangled and looking not unlike an outdated combine harvester, set aside. My mother's tears are rolling to meet the twilit rye. And when the word *flee* is used, it normally entails something more boxy than the blowing trench coat coattails conjured: fake papers, battered suitcases full of random, utmost precious things, the last train out of here. The Wall, which like other things my mother held to be immutable, was not.

Also in the revolution:
façade-dragged and behold, beheaded:
the price of bread henceforth is fixed and

we shall rename all the

days.

Pull time from its appointed slots and it shall run in grooves of ten from here on in – this we wish our freedom form to take.
(In the end they were mistaken: these were not the kings of France but those of Judah)

Lola's family's lawyer had the name of Ferdinand Marcos.
Depending on who she's speaking to, Lola will say with pride that the
getaway car for his wedding was loaned by the family;
or that it was my great-grandmother's shoe collection that gave
Imelda the idea for her three thousand pairs of shoes.
         (My great-grandmother did not have three thousand pairs of shoes)
But to me she will say:
Caridad (my great-grandmother, she of the jade and pearls and the
cigarette holder and the dining table which could seat sixty)
she was outspoken against him, and she
held open house each and every Sunday and 'fostered conversation'
(among dissidents, journalists, friends)
and though this was martial law and like many other places in this
century, a time of nights where black cars could come slinking to snitch
you for the secret police
they never dared touch her.

There was English, in the clerestory of my mouth. There was French, stowed in the front of my lower jaw. My father spoke Spanish, which was slippery on the tongue and the teeth like a series of smooth stones. And then there was German, that language my parents peddled between them like a secret. It was hairy, like a wild pig, and came lumbering from the back of the throat. When I was five I told my mother that American was a sideways language. French and English were perpendiculars.

Words are for things and some words are the truest possible expression of the thing. For instance: *vielleicht, gourmand, moist.*

French was a series of tight-skinned drums I needed to hit quickly in turn.
English was round in the middle and sometimes closed, sometimes open, at ends.

There are some words that tether me more strongly to themselves and therefore the world. What do they do with their one inadequate language? What moors them?

My father spoke Tagalog until he was five. All that is lost now. He knows only the monsoon sounds of that season attendant upon his most unpromised birth. There is that lilt in it that sounds like the saddle of the afternoon, before the sky splits like the belly of a fruit.

(Note how I could have said *like the belly of an overripe fruit* or *like the belly of a rotting fruit*. But to do so would have been toddling into the tintypes you draw on when you think of those places encompassed by the tropical clime as being stultifying, cloying in their fertility, somehow unclean even in that you see them as a possibility for plunder. Did you know? That the colonised mass is often configured as a female body – the Americas as luring one in and revealing their dangers later; Africa as dark and sinister and the utmost alluring in inscrutability. And in my meetings with people, often is the assumption that it is my mother who is the Filipina.
Please explain.)

The Cebuano for 'I don't know' translates as 'it is not within my head'.

A baby brother, all for me.

The house where we were born had a deck like a ship which fell away to the ocean and the city, spiky in glass. There was a brown dog with a wag-wag dactylic tail. Our parents were strong and enormous, like giant sequoias.

You will recall I told you it had been a grey morning? Well perhaps you will be aware how London light at October time flashes sometimes gold and bright.

My parents ran away west when they saw their friends bowing out of life against ills and back into the Home Counties.
There were weddings which affirmed this,
on the mornings of an English May
with dresses crisp as meringues –
so they ran, to California, which is where you go
when you want
to get close
to the edge.

The world here is rolling into its third millennium. My mother is wearing a tiny white dress and kissing my father. She beckons me to taste champagne, and it prickles. Across the world my grandfather is coughing. This time the thing in his lungs cannot be drained.

This was in what would become the Benighted States
when on a clear blue day with a scrap of smog above the bay
a fourth plane destined for SFO –

when I was six
twin planes flew into the great glass cathedral.
This cathedral followed the particular structure
of the High Gothic,
namely the towers as a forward face, placed to match the
westward-waning sun-path
but was built for a more certain, though equally volatile, god.
My mother hid it from us for a year.
All those nights of news
the magazine covers everywhere
all my classmates drawing flaming planes in afternoon drawing time
until, a year later, in an airport giftshop,
a coffee table book of photos from the day, and my brother asking
But Mummy, were there people on the plane?

The things you keep of dead people are funny: a shoebox full of his old-fashioned bow ties no one will wear, but I have a theory my mother keeps them, up on the shelf with the hats for weddings, because of the smell; or the signet ring with the crest worn off, cut from his dead finger, or the pictures of lion statues in a box-file, that he collected with views to who knows.

I remember him dying. I remember him of us unremembering because they shot him full of morphine. I remember the purple hyacinth in a pot in the waiting room of the hospital in Nîmes. I remember how my mother went away for the first time when he began to die. I remember her sleeping on a cot in his room (she told me later this was because he had nightmares and hallucinations and, having lifelong slept naked, he would run into the street and point to the sky and say: They're coming!). I remember the people who came – English people I was told were related to me. I remember taking a plate of pink grapefruit up to him in his bedroom. Before he died I remember his Kipling and King James, the nicotine thunder of him as I sat on his lap. At his funeral I remember my grandmother's voice cracking. We were not allowed to wear black, so my mother wore white and my father wore blue and I wore a green dress and my brother wore white with grey. It had been my sixth birthday three days before, so I had taken my sequin handbag with me and every time we stood up or sat down (my brother's and my first time in a church) I would open it and look inside, because this is what I felt grown-up women did. Later, my brother would ask me why we stood up and sat down so much, and I said, *Because the seats are so uncomfortable.*

My mother had been told that although these were dark days, she would have some of the best conversations of her life with her father. But she did not, because he became determined to receive a pardon (regarding the frocking) from Rome. Much paperwork was done to sort out his damnation, and soon enough the Pope himself forgave him, and four days later my grandfather died. Clearing out afterwards, my mother gave away the antique crucifix that had hung always over his bed.

THE MINUTES OF THE 133RD ANNUAL GENERAL MEETING OF
THE ASSOCIATION OF THE VENERABLE COLLEGE OF SAINT
THOMAS DE URBE (THE ROMAN ASSOCIATION)
HELD AT THE RAVEN HOTEL, DROITWICH
TUESDAY 4 JUNE 2002
4) Deceased members The *De Profundis* was prayed for the repose of the souls of , , ; , , ; David Collier; , , ; , , ; , , and all members who had died since the previous meeting.
(A song of ascents. From the depths I have called you)
(*The Venerabile*, 2002, vol. xxxii, no. 3)

In the hospital he was strapped to the bed by his wrists.

The day he died our mother dropped my brother and I off with family friends and we swam naked in their pool.
(If our nudity leaps out at you as an odd detail, know that I include it to be
    indicative of the fact that she forgot our swimming trunks; she left fast.)
When our mother came back from the hospital at lunch,
the call came from Nana that he had died.
I do not remember being told.
Curtis and Marina sat her down and would not let her
leave until she had eaten something. It will not matter,
they told her, if you get there half an hour or
an hour after it has happened,

but you must eat something.
So she did.

What do you eat, when you know that sixteen or so
kilometres from you, the body of your father
grows colder by the minute and lies
strapped to a bed by its wrists?

You must eat now, because later you will forget, they told her.

Then she got in the car and drove.
The road is long, largely flat, with groves of olive trees on either side,
and a wide expanse to the left which stretches away towards salt farms
and then the sea.
She says that she started driving and then she cried and cried and cried,
and while she cried she felt his presence all around her:
in the car and in the sky, and hovering just above the hills and the road
and she prayed as she had never prayed in her life before or since,
that if heaven was there, that it take him, that it take good care of him,
that it make him feel welcome and keep him safe.

It was the ides of July, and so the heat would have wavered and parted
over the road,
and the trees would have thronged with scores of cicadas strumming their
wings.
There would have been a hot, dry, wind smelling of coniferous trees.
The afternoon sun would have bounced off the tarmac.

I think of my mother, driving bare-armed in a sleeveless scarlet shirt, with a tortoiseshell hair slide and tortoiseshell sunglasses, and her long gold-auburn hair beating in the headrest's slipstream.

My grandmother and my grandfather are driving to the hospital in Tripoli.
The road from Misrata.
The bare ground. The hospital garden. The nuns who rescued gazelles.
Nana did some of the driving.
I did some of the driving.
The director of the hospital:
Mrs Collier, you have had a baby girl? Come back next year and have a boy.
No, thank you.
No anaesthetic, no incubator. The rising desert sun.
She shielded her baby with her hands.
The late theatre of an imperial war.
Italy. Tobruk.
The souk in Tunisia where gold was sold by weight.
For his wife twin bangles.
At the end they did not love each other.
Surprisingly, her voice cracked and the bangles clanged on the coffin.
It was decided we would move to France.

After the planes flew into the high towers, two countries which claimed me joined one another in invasion. And the country I would grow into would not. And the country of my birth outraged. After everything we did for them in 1940! (shouted our neighbour across the street, in his house of redwood and plate glass).
French wine flowed through the streets (because people had poured it there, in protest and disgust).

(This flowing of the wine is often summoned as the single most salient
detail in France's refusal to go to war. Not only by my parents.)

The Parthenon Galleries
the screaming Horse of Selene:
Mother, Father, you move in processional
monumental, hacked of your origins to be enshrined in this museum I
have made
a cathedral for all my colonialisms
Mama, Papa, names I have not called you –
you rank among the finest achievements of Ancient Assyrian art
I have gathered up all the shards you offered
Look!
I have built you a cathedral
you are my mother and my father
you shall be eternal as the broken pieces of Elgin's grand tour
acanthus-furled corinthian
ionic ironic iconic.
In the museum also there will be the mythologies I will make –
the redwood trees, how they smelled in fog.

The sphinx has wings at times
and devoured those who could not unriddle
and yet

       died

          at the successful uncoupling of her meaning from its shades;
a slaughter of interpretation so rightwing, pedantic,

                                       (masculine.)
Scripture is not the text but that which erases its own interpretation.

    Mama, Papa, look
    I have torn it all down
    to make you a museum!

    (in the space between my lungs
    the dark leathery wings grew bigger
    – a darkly deploying enemy crouching –
    till they began to beat
    drawing my breath away)

            (if I do not build you the museum   they will kill me.)

It was a grey day, March; raining pathetically. Mummy was wearing beige
and something the colour of dried blood. She parked on the main street
of our French grey town and went inside the Analyses Medicales (I would
read this later, and know). She looked beautiful.
She came tripping back through the grey wet, got into the driver's seat,
and turned around.
'Guess what?' She grinned.
It was a game. Mummy is my best friend. I smiled back. I said:
'What?'
'I'm pregnant.'

(I became acutely aware of the car smelling of car; and of the ugly trees
and the rain runnelling off the windows. Something boomed. For months
I dreamed I pinned and punched her until she miscarried. In the days
afterwards I would ask her to 'get rid of it' and 'flush it out'. In the months
before it was born I did not want her to hold me. If she cuddled me I went
limp. I didn't want to go home with her from school. I tried to get lost
at the supermarket. I hid in a wardrobe when she called me for dinner.
I spent afternoons after school reading under my bed. She said it was
Daddy's idea. She said it was an accident, which was a lie and I couldn't
figure out why she told it. She smiled weakly when people asked if I was
excited and I said no. All the early pictures are of my brother holding
the baby. I would fall asleep with the crumpled wish inside my fists that
when I woke up all the baby things would be gone and it would have been
a dream. When she was maybe a week old I came down the stairs one
afternoon and saw the reflection of Mummy playing with her, speaking
the blithering language of the baby-besotted, and I carried on down the
hallway into the kitchen where someone had left the carving knife on a
chopping board. I stood looking at the knife and listening to the language
in the room, and I thought about how easy it would be to lock myself in
the bathroom and fill the sink with warm water. I was nine. I do not know
if that is a memory I made up.)

Her face changed. Her smile was the smile of a stupid person.

There must have been something wrong with me.
'Uh-oh.'
She laughed, then there was a flash of frown.

When she was first born she bored me. She was ugly and didn't do much. She made squeaking noises with my mother's nipple in her mouth and when you took off her clothes she was mottled and purple. She smelled of sour milk always; I had an urge to rip the crusty nub of umbilical cord off her.

This new sister was blonde, with blue eyes;
She was sweet, she was kind, she was uncomplicatedly happy.
Her answers never embarrassed.

Part II: Narthex

(Y)
I am the bracketed why
The W? XY said
I am the α: u bet
the c u next
I am the body of the text.

I am the why
in French: Greek I
the lone line self
upright probe and pelvic cradle
splay me open for an X
mark the spot with sex
hang the sheets out to dry

Of Canterbury I recall
scuff
stone smell
shoe seep
smell at crotch of tights
'blazer'.

To the school: I am delivered. A three-hour drive north, through a valed
land replete with cathedrals. There is Amiens, with its traces of paint, still;
and Chartres of the windows; Beauvais, unfinished – three times its spire
fell through; now it is braced with wooden beams: on crutches. It boasts
the highest clerestory in Europe, it smells of mouldering stone. Rheims
where are buried the kings; Coulombs which boasts the foreskin of the
Saviour. Under the Channel, to burst forth near a hill where runs a horse
white in chalk.

(I remember that boat, smallest to answer the call.)

(Named Tamzine, it lies on the floor of the museum for imperial war.)

(The littlest of the little ships of Dunkirk,

clinker-built from Canadian spruce.)

The school is of flint and brick, it too has a cathedral.

At the boarding house, which is new, but built out of the ruins of the old
infirmary ten centuries old, another mother is wearing a poncho. She asks
where we're from, how we got here. At my mother's reply (the Eurotunnel)
she says *Oh well you will have come in under our land then*.

I am unpacked and stowed away.

Later that night, the others start to arrive. There are five blondes in a total of twelve. There is lacrosse gear and lurid pink mouthguards. Their jeans are different from mine (tighter). I have never seen so many sets of big breasts. Their hair is mid-length (it swishes). Their clothes are all somehow the same.

– Are you rich?

(The others wait politely for my reply)

The land seemed so old, but deluded also.
The white horse that leaps on the green hill, singing in chalk,
is a copy.
The stone of the cathedral came from Caen, where as a child in an oversized fleece
I stood in a very large crater near the Museum of Peace.
'My father was at D-Day and was shot in the hip, he lay on the beach in the surf for three days.'
My godfather has my baby sister strapped to his chest.
This cool cold plain of Europe's beige edge is on par with Mont St Michel, its
great flat-footed expanse where my brother and I dig its ridges for clams before the tide
comes running.
This is deep bone-knowing country.

Albion.

I hold it in my mouth with pleasure like a corp
ulent pearl.
It contains all the stories England tells itself:
a plosive, bounded space, girded by neat cliffs and land's end.
How they thought of their virgin queen,
the whole universe under her skirts.

The dean beckoned me and with his thumb
Upon my forehead said *admitto te*
And I having for sole reference the Simba smudge, stumbled on the stiff
white surplice lent to me on a two-year lease.

They were so blithe about the signifiers of their station. They had hairless
pits and thighs, and paid, from the age of not yet fucking or fingering, for
bikini waxes. They had an easy greed and met me with incomprehension
when I tried in vain to explain where I came from.

Food was a thing ingested under mild duress.

My femalehood was boarded over my eyes like a set piece.
To determine its deviance became the all-consuming aim.
Cover your shoulders.
Shoulders remind boys of boobs.
My body became as incendiary as a vernacular.
It was the thing that lay in the dark woods at the trailing ends of
sentences,
at the short edge of night and late at skirt.

The blonde others aspired to be described with mean, hard-nosed little
words: thin, pretty, nice.
I wanted big-femur words like wise and kind.

The boys were always
touching
each other.

When the parents came, they were loud.
They came two by two in pairs of Sunday-lunching racists.
The fathers wore trousers the colour of rare meat.

(A hunk of roast beef seeping)
(banking on things in the city)
(with flats, useful for unfaithing.)

Their wives stayed at home, in the counties. Maybe they were lonely, and screamed
themselves hoarse in the cut-stone quiet of their houses.
These marriages seemed structures of mutual scorn.
Watching them made me flush hot with fear that this was coming for me
and sent me knock-kneed to hide.
Their days of Barbour-ed torpor; the cream-coloured afternoons –

I wanted big-beamed love. I wanted to be one of the women who swear
and have grey in their hair. I wanted, though this too was warped, to be
the emotional centre without which nothing can hold.

In our lesson the time-lined people have made landfall in America. The
people they find there are untime-lined, according to the landfalls they
have no history. This is something that even the ancients did not know.
This is something entirely new. Everything is uncertain. The world is of
unknown proportions. Luther is nailing a piece of paper to a door. He is
standing saying I stand before you now and can do no other. Everything is
chaos. Nothing is known. The universe is a black womb rioting with stars.

On the staircase in the history block was a framed print
WE SHALL FIGHT THEM ON THE BEACHES
all around it dotted coats of arms and rays of light, which seemed a slight
confusion.

In the paintings which depict the lead-up to Becket's braining,
he looks so meek.

(I bet he wasn't)

His brocade all leafy and trefoiled roundabout his shoulders,
ready as a rosette with his palms held pressing,
but only just apart for that
self-touching
prayer,
so erotic.

How much
I would have liked
to have been first to thumb-flick a flame
and behold the stamping procession of beasts
at Lascaux or Chauvet.
How I would have liked
to know that fear.
To see those who had professed
with smudge of opposable thumbs.
The paintings had been sleeping, stoppered up
for sixty thousand years
it is said they were so fresh, after the finding
there was still charcoal dust.
It is the same
as standing in the transept
itching in a cassock

(it enrages people when I say
I served in the cathedral
because I liked the costume)

holding frankincense
in a gravy boat
watching as below
atomised taper-flame spread up through the nave
and at the back a lone voice rising

in the dark:
this too like a thumb on stone.

A ruddy smudge in the bridge of my knickers (one of the truly good
English words). I thought:
'I have begun to bleed. Perhaps I am a woman now.'

There was a history paper entitled BRITISH FOREIGN POLICY OF THE
19TH CENTURY, sponsored by the board of English education. It stopped
at 1890. Through its opiate emissions it fed them sugar-pills of who they
were. This was also the time when the first queen regnant to give birth did
so and with her many-fruited womb once again was emblematic of the
pink stain on an atlas third. I saw that it was dangerous to subscribe.

(Roll your skirt up at the waist.)

Lifesize statues of a naked man with our sightlines up his loincloth.
Surplices smoothing over tits.
We were made to carry hymnbooks in blue and gold, which had some
variation on:
JESUS IS HOT
FUCK
(_)
_____-) – – – –
(_)
In four-way biro: green.

They were confirmed so as to be gifted hoops and cufflinks of white gold.
Common prayers.
They wanted to marry in squat flint churches, as if they were tourists, with
big white dresses, as if they were cakes.

Once a month came round
the metallic, zincish smell in the corridors, of all our clumping blood in
bins.

In the run of evenings the flatline pallid blue shaded to plum,
the cathedral kept thrusting up: centripetal, unrenounced.
I am English en-lessoned. We are being taught 'The Flea'.
This flea is you and I, and this
Our marriage bed... w'are met,
And cloistered in these living walls of jet
I think of a bed: one of those little beds, short and tight in stately homes.
Thick-curtained against the cold. This seemed to me at the time of my
buttressing in pinstripes, to be something rich and strange I wished to
know.
buttress, *n.*: a structure of stone or brick built against a wall to strengthen
or support it
buttress, *v.*: increase the strength or justification for; reinforce.
In the great age of cathedrals, flying buttresses were instated to counteract
the lateral forces of high walls and naves, which would seek to burst open.
They were like ribs –
A universe so newly heliocentric. How afraid he must have been.

There is a word that appears only six times in our language, *banhus*
meaning bone-house. This is called a kenning, a word only a hundred
and fifty years old. It comes from the Old Norse *kenna*, to know, to
perceive. If I were to ask my mother she would say that German *kennen*
is for knowledge that is already within, and *wissen* is for knowledge
that enters. *Ken* is excused of empiricism. In Old English scholarship,
a kenning is a compound word, but a purposefully poetic one; it is a
metaphor compressed. Thus a bone-house is a body. A house made of
bones is like a great hall in the time before cathedrals, beam-ribbed.

My body is a hall on a hill in the dark.

Give me a life of bleeding on your behalf!

I had teachers who nudged me towards the open hungry vowels of the
marrow-cracking class
and led me to literature, which was a great fridge in the middle of the
night and I was starving,

                                    (sixteen and straining in my pinstripes).

So I came to texts, and those who have been appointed to tell us what they
mean. I sympathised with those spined creatures we split open on desks,
discerning their dispossessed. Jesus was in everything; a bore.

Then there was
Rest your human head, my love
(how often I would think of that in the grey half-heart of a Wednesday
dawning)

At the school I learned:
to twist praise and to deflect it always
that boys were *growing men* with *needs*
that I was disgusting and, at best, allegorical.

At events I was made to stand in-stalled in a sundress and smilingly scoop
up clotted cream to fathers who wore no wedding rings.

Lesson:
In the lift there is one man.
We are standing diametrically opposed
across the textured linoleum mat.
This is how he tells me
he won't strangle me in this shut
shaft-shuttling box.
He is being demonstrable.
He hates me that he has to.

Kick pleat.

On Monday nights, we changed our bedding. In the boys' houses, this was done for them.

The new headmaster instated that girls were not allowed into the dining hall unless their legs were covered.

These are the things I was promised I would one day desire: mortgage, marriage, questions about procreation, obfuscation of fornication. Such teleologies are not for the wicked, but are reserved for the good. These being, for the avoidance of doubt: the people with children, in owned houses, gardens, and plenty of mugs. Drive, with gate (spiked). Kitchen island, antique china. My mother wanted these things. She had not had them, so I understand.

A church education will teach you that the monopoly of interpretation is just.

I was to be prepared for a life of profit and no empathy.

Over the rubbish truck-rutted tarmac there streaks a plane or a moth or a floodlit bird.
This is not an alignment for a king, this is not the portent of Troy.
There will be no annunciation here.
There is only this tongue in my mouth.

> Ransomed healed restored forgiven
> To our fathers in distress
> Slow to chide and swift to bless
> Fatherlike, he tends and spares us
> Bow down before him now
> in reverence and fear.

The darkness deepens
From sea to shining sea

Assembly in the flat midwinter bleak of Kent. We are all ensconced in
rows.
'Eve,' begins the Professor, who is American and says what *hwat*, like –
as later I would learn – the first line of *Beowulf*
'– should be taken as a role model'
Hwæt! We Gardena in geardagum
so begins the first story in our language: Listen!
We the Spear-Danes in days of yore
but it sounds like We of the garden, who asked what and why –
'– because she dared to seize the unknown.'
Thanet: the landing of Brutus, and also glass houses for growing tomatoes
(Geography)
Whitstable: St Augustine, and oysters (in months with an R)
Margate: T. S. Eliot connecting nothing with his broken fingernails
We of the garden in the days of yore: listen
'Eve was the first intellectual.'
He said this in the cathedral school at Canterbury. He was never asked to
speak again.
Later
Paradise Lost. 'The word for knowledge and the word for taste have the
same root' says the woman in blue boots – 'to taste is to know'.
To taste is to know
and to know biblically is to consume/ate
Like *savoir* and *savourer*, to know and to take pleasure in tasting
homo sapiens, man of knowledge, knowing man
I wanted to know a man.

> (there is a pull
> in my thighs
> like a tide)

I fidgeted at their hollow faith.
While at our remembrance service we hymned
we were pilgrims in this place.
We were adversarial, like gladiators,
and bony, like foals.

> (but! Comparison of horses to women is a cheap trick,
> devised by those who prefer the company of horses)

The girls fascinated me more. They worked hard to marry well.
None of them envisaged working beyond the age of thirty,
when they wanted to *become mums*

> (as if knighted)
>
> (and then, maybe at a later date, become primary school teachers).

Summer of sixteen, season of denim cut-offs.
The stories trickled back to us:
Helen had sex *in a field!*
Frances and Ben had sex *eight times!*
It was, most definitely, a race.
Side partings, for hiding.
Centre partings, for the brave.
Head was not something girls received.
Instead, they were licked *out.*
These had to be carefully managed:
no sucking or you were condemned.
Knowing the smells, we said *I don't think I would ever let a guy lick me out.*
It's so gross down there.
But I hear it's great.
It's meant to be amazing,
Never give a guy a handjob! He will always be better at it than you.
They would suck their own dicks if they could.
Giving head is *so* gross.
How long does an erection take?

Does the dick slip out sometimes?
We passed copies of *Cosmo* round.
Give him a view which is truly X-rated
The Stair Sizzler
The day after, it was so painful I couldn't sit down!
I bled so much! Luckily I was wearing a red playsuit!
What happens if you fart?
No one told you that the cum comes back out again.

Miss, did God rape Mary?
What?
Did God rape Mary?
What makes you say that?

(We are reading Yeats's 'Leda and the Swan'.)

Because Zeus raped Leda!
And?
I have seen the paintings of the scene. Leda lying, her skin like big blobs of
mist. Always seeming somehow so uncontained, leaky, porous, dissolute.
The matter of her. What of it. And the swan, so beaky, with its big sharp
feathers splayed and the snaky neck between her legs.
In the paintings of Mary reading (could she read?) in the garden, before
the news of it is to hit her, the Holy Ghost is often depicted as a small,
pointy-looking finch or something, zooming like a fighter jet towards her
chest in a spiky ray of light, and Gabe the Enabler standing quietly by.
Her hand going slack on the board. My theory loosed and petulant. Her
mind and mouth a momentary blank. Nothing. What could she say, on
that clear day with the finial shadow play on the bold-bordered quad of
initiate green?

Further in *Beowulf* there is the *sceadu-genga*, *scriðian*, or: *the shadow-foe comes creeping.*

(This *scriðian* is a sort of slithering, but also a gliding and could involve flight.)

Grendel grows angry at seeing the great hall Heorot lit from within:
he aches with unknowing at the warmth of wine shared

Grendel goes largely undescribed. We know he has an arm because
Beowulf tears it off and nails it to the door.
We know that his eyes are *leoht unfæger*, lit from within, and grim,
meaning also *holding hellfire*, but perhaps only reflecting the lamps
already in the hall.
And he is *mearcstapa*, one who treads at edges.

They tried to hide the violence which would come to us.
They hinted, but at the kind which was granular,
concerning only our bodies,
but even then always vaguely, never using the words.
Male violence was most certainly physical, and confined to a
certain class.

The churchliness of it all was a lie,
 a cladding wall, partition, counterfeit. It always felt slightly apologetic
about the religiosity of its own message, so sermons came to us cloaked
in Harry Potter and raspberry jelly.
No, I am not joking.
A cult of self-control and cold water,
cleats and a rapacious virtue in which we had no place.
They did not know what to do with us, so told us all the obvious
outrageous things, grievances which I carry to you now in armfuls
and lay at your feet.

My mother went to school in this country to learn about England, where she was from: how it worked, the stuff it was made of. She said she had none of the slang.

Lola was sent to boarding school near Hastings. A many-legged journey from Manila: to Saigon, Phnom Penh, Bangkok, New Delhi, Karachi (disembarking for showers in barracks), Teheran, Athens, Rome, Paris, London, down over twilled English fields, craning to see the cows – standing or sitting? – and the swallows – swooping high or swooping low? This stretch of English selvedge. The rain perpetual, and barbiturate. Guillaume le Bâtard forever coming over the hill. Head girl at her table in the dining hall: suet pudding, bread pudding, rice pudding, spotted dick.

'The first year, there was an English girl whose father worked with Cable & Wireless and she had grown up in Malaysia. I remember her very well because she knew how to pick up things on the floor with her toes, like me.' (I used to do this, not knowing where the habit came from. Little hints, made manifest. I don't know when I lost it.)

My father first fell away from the church aged fifteen.

Mount St Mary's. Jesuits in Yorkshire. My father has been sent here to get away from Barcelona, and the Austrian. He is destined to be head boy, to be termed a *nutter* at rugby. He loves it here.

There is some incident wherein Lola runs from Barcelona, flies to England and drives to Mount St Mary's to come get him. Lola in a rented car, driving across a moor that falls away in heather-scrubbed expanse on either side. Her perfect shellacked hands steely upon the wheel.

She tells him she is leaving the Austrian; to come with her. I do not know where they thought they would go. Lola is thirty-five. But then: she is pregnant. So she leaves without him.

My father finds out like this: one of the Jesuits pulls him aside to say *your mother is doing the right thing by going back to her husband.*

He had others who loved him in this time, namely

Stéphanie, Lola's dear friend from secretarial school, and her husband Paul,

Paul's mother had been heiress to a rubber plantation in what was then Indochina. She had stood pregnant while it burned.

Et moi, Paul told us, *quand j'étais petit, pendant la guerre, on me mettait du nước mắm dans mon biberon, pour les vitamines.*

Years later, living a plaster-moulding life in Paris, Paul's mother would go for dinner in a Vietnamese restaurant, enquire as to the legitimacy of a fish dish, saying:

     – We did not have this when I was in Indochina.

To which the Vietnamese waitress replied:

     – No, we came up with this after you left.

April. I, the child, tugging at the hem of all that my father had made for
me.
A sea-frayed edge of Scotland. Looking for universities.
There was a beach.
When I was tiny, there was a beach with sea glass. I filled my pockets until
my yellow mac sagged. A time when my immortal parents strode on the
sand.

Siehst, Vater, du den Erlkönig nicht?

Here I filled my pockets, but some of the glass was still sharp so my palm
lines became cross-hatched red.
This was an end. I stared at the sea. It was raining.

Mein Vater, mein Vater, und hörest du nicht,
was Erlenkönig mir leise verspricht?

Father, do not take this literally,
but stranded on the sands of St Andrews
on the eighteenth of April in the year twenty-twelve,
you strangled me.
I wanted to walk into the sea
with my clothes full of stones.

(At the sacking of Lindisfarne,
the gospels go wrapped in blankets.)

My father
had snapped under the habitual insult
of rearing a woman.

And he was suddenly enraged

afterwards his hands slammed down onto my shoulders:
I am sorry I came down so hard on you.

Mein Vater, mein Vater, jetzt faßt er mich an
Erlkönig hat mir ein Leids getan!

                           (the shadow-foe had slither-snatched him too)

To come to the Grail Chapel and find it empty:
the door creaked off its hinge
a fern grew in the cliff cleft,

                        (like the vents of the Roquefort caves
                          where they grow cheese in vats in the dark)
this absence had not even the noblesse oblige of a void
those derelict mushrooms made me want to lie down in the sea.

He'd left the door ajar, just long enough for me to see
the beatings, the shoutings, the things that were hinted at
on the rare occasions when my mother mentioned them, driving in Paris
grey.
Saying I think he sees now how she was brave in her own way.
Lola at that point (my childhood, us not long in France) still married to
this man, this grey, cragged-up man I will never meet, this ghoul who
flares up in my father's rage and scares him, hard.
And then he shut the door and guided me away with a hand on my back.

I did not want the future I felt I had been put forward for, a sentiment
which I mismanaged and hurt my mother with. She cried, she was so
insulted. My father glared. There were holes in their logic. They were
wrong, and they'd never been wrong before. The ground cracked out from
under me. I made plans to run away, or kill myself. In the end I ran a
penknife down my arm to see what it would feel like (it left a tiny thread of
scab), went back to school, and didn't e-mail for a while.

At one point in Heorot, Hrothgar's queen emerges, passes round a cup or horn, and retreats again to some unknowable room. This female space which the text knows better than to touch; I like to think of existing there, in its quiet outside reach.

It is estimated that three quarters of this period's literature has been lost. But how to quantify the unknown? When our tutor told us of Sutton Hoo I questioned her in circles about the boat, the memory of the boat, a boat, of boat-wood, its trace, in the ground. How does the ground know to remember?

I began to denounce the dialectic of deodorant ads.

What is a woman?
An irrevocable invitation to interpretation.

What is a book?
An invitation to identify.

What is a cathedral?
A show of force.

Who was Tamara of the Goths?
One who was too hungry.

What is an island?
A thing of limits,
which likes to think it knows
where it begins and ends
not bleeding into others

a tamper-evident opening
tear here

the egregious arrogance of this self-ensconcing country!

The meaning which couches inside me
the meaning which slouches beside me

This sacred crossing place.
I do not want your non-committal creed thank you.

What did I learn there?
To veily loathe the office of my gender
and all others who held it.

Who were those who walked among us?
Who ran on the brittle bones of not enough love
and consequently, broke femurs.
When we knew them, their teeth got greyer from the Diet Coke and bile;
they went bow-legged with the effort:
their shins like the gentle curves of cricket bats,
their many silver rings shuttled back and forth on notchy knuckles,
their hair went dull and their ovaries, like stunted seedlings, never grew.
Their mothers (happy with their sons) did not love them, and their fathers
knew not what to do.

It was happening to all of us. Our parents like pediments falling
I heard the wails through the duvet-padded walls of the laundry room.

The Enthronement of the One Hundred and Fifth Cantuarian Archbishop

Blue and purple sliver fish dancing on his amethyst-carbuncled cloak and his crozier like a giant hairpin, its alabaster-coloured hook. We barred and shut the doors. He banged with his crozier and justified his ask to enter.
Who are you and why do you request entry?
I come as one seeking, to travel with you.
Why have you come to us?
I have been sent.
How do you come among us, and with what confidence?
I come knowing nothing.
That glory may dwell in this land! We have looked forward to your coming with great joy.

> (He was seated in St Augustine's chair, St A of the highly significant abbey where Milly B fucked Benedict D nightly, she said the altar was most sheltered from the wind.)

Let us greet our new archbishop with great gladness!
Afterwards, in the chapter house, we scholars, a surpliced sampling, were required to swear allegiance to him, a vow one hundred and five archbishops old. But him having refused to relinquish his views on marriage equality (*some gay couples have loving, stable and monogamous relationships of 'stunning' quality*, according to him at the time) and the dean being a *non-practising gay man*, I looked Justin in the eye and declined to give him the Latin that had been put into my hands, which I would have not known how to say anyway.
One night, towards the end (when I could afford, increasingly, to laugh at them openly):

> – all dwarves look the same
> – what?

     – yeah, like, to the untrained eye, all Asians look alike
     – yes, it's easier to differentiate between Black people
I tugged hard on a sharp laugh
     – Stephanie is ethnic, this upsets her more
(I did it again, this red cord conversationally dangling)
(Their names, improbably, rhymed)
and no nurse came tap-tap running down the corridor to administer.

When the United States came knocking for its foothold in the ironically
named Pacific in 1903
a member of my family was swindled of some several thousand hectares
near Subic Bay
for an airbase which would be named for the clean-jawed Clark.
Wherefrom was eventually waged most of the bombing of Vietnam,
Cambodia, and Laos.
Historians refer to the base as having been a *backbone of logistical support*
for Kissinger's crimes.

Nine hours after what happened at Pearl Harbor,
Clark Field would be bombed and subsequently overrun
like time running over, like water flowing over a cup.
If you are familiar with the name Douglas MacArthur, HQ'd here at the
butting-place, you should know also of the names and their lilts, linked
like a necklace of beads across the dateline
in the order of the dawn: Wake, Guam, Davao, Baguio.
MacArthur getting off lightly, giving his name to transit stops
and avenues,
and us to this day gummy in our ignorance

                                                of Guam.

Part III: Hapax Legomena

– So your mum is Filipino?

– *A*. Filipin*a* if you're a woman. Like Latina. Same empire.

– So your mum is Filipina?

– No, my dad.

– Oh.

– Where are you from?

My reply, only as of late:

– I'm British but was born in the States and grew up in France. And I'm half Filipina.

– Oh OK wow. So your mum is half Filipina?

– Where are you from?

– pffffffffffffffffffffff.

– Where are you from?

– My mother is British but grew up in West Germany and my father is Filipino but grew up in Spain and they met here but had me in California and then moved to France and now I am here.

– Oh OK wow.

– Where are you from?

– My grandmother on my dad's side is Filipina but was exiled to Spain for getting pregnant and my grandfather on my mum's side was a Catholic priest and there is a gap in the story the story resumes when he has been defrocked and they are married and they fled the scandal to Libya to be teachers and my mother was born there and from there they went to West Germany and my parents met here but left when their friends turned back into their English upper middle class parents so went to California and there they had me but then they moved to France where we lived for 11 years and now I am here.

– Oh OK wow

Oh
OK
wow

No room in their view for people like me.

Student nights with their divine time of bells and the bloodbeats of other bodies.

I saw the sum of love my parents came from, and I wanted
  a piece
    of that.

Catchment areas, not pertaining to rivers. Lotteries, not pertaining to winning great sums. All that money lurking in the walls of houses. We were casting around for angles of oppression to cling to and be perpetually enraged.

Postcolonial
Postcode

    (lottery)

Post imperial
We were learning, with great viciousness, to unzip one another of our illusions.

It was my turn with collisions.

On a bus lurching through plane trees I kissed a boy whose mouth
tasted of ashes

We come to one another like flotsam on the tides of work and day, to be
made gentle, to be made gritty, by the pints we wash upon ourselves.
Sitting on the sticky seats of pubs we laugh and prod and pry.
Consequently we speak of sex with a slippery and eager ease, and money:
rent, train fares, the price of living and avocados. We are
discerning the things most deserving of our virtue.
None is more deserving than virtue itself.
Our chickens reassure us that they come from trusted farms.
Sometimes the conversations are arousing in the dexterity of their
structure, and sometimes they are like a game whose rules I cannot
grasp, they move too fast and are too mean for me to understand.
Sometimes they want to go in big raucous groups to a curry house
    (The establishment of choice when white people want to behave badly.
        In one, Emma's cheek was cut by a samosa which had been thrown.)

Compline after sex, for acoustic effect
never went again after all the imploration.
Felt cleaner letting all the semen
fall back out
again

In those years
I gave my sleep to pale boys
and stroked their whiteness amazed.

My hybridity confused.
I was stand-in for
that which was not.
I was clutched as proof
a talisman against their own circumstantial failings
and in this way we were all absolved.

And then I was Petrarch in Avignon,
hit with the slap of it, like a fish:
no one told me about the men who would come,
wanting to carry me off into their lives;
No! I would scream

         myself raw on the beach.

The shy men I held
tried to shake from years of tweed sleep
who swam in the language of the fathers with ease
(others, perpetually in exile, cannot)

We rolled each other over and kissed
shoulders and nape and sacrum
the plate within
strongest in all the body

(on their spines,
skin was stretched sticky over blanks
where women should have been.)

They had big purple stretchmarks on the sides of their hips.
Starking out in high relief
where their little bodies had shot apart fast.

It is the time after
after the cut-up cold
bodies
which run in friezes on the wall.
Orthogonalising
in the museum that says

                Please Do Not Touch.

The orthogonals of your bodies become
panathenaic in a frieze of forms:
all my sleepers
who have passed through the duck-egg rooms like a breeze, leaving little
plaques,
some of you I dredged from the sea.

We lie like brackets
enclosing a pause:

our children as yet unsummoned

from the blue hiatus.

This bed
conjugat
with all our writhing verbs.

I shall love you
in the margins of the day.

I contain
all those anecdotal crumbs passed over vestiged meals when they
impressed their cloisonné mythologies: 9/11, World War One, Battle of
Britain, rationing, résistance, Russians coming. I contain the creed and
cadence of King James and though I did not wish for this I bring it to(o)

Our mothers speaking from within their own wave
taught us the deferral of hope
                                        (much the only way America sustains itself.)
The promise of eventuals yawns out over the horizon: linear, vectoral,
leaving us behind.

There is a book hanging upside down between my lungs like a bat.

When musing on how beauty differs
a common case study is the binding of feet in imperial China.

Do not be an idiot says my mother raking the fire,
it is to stop them from running away.

> (The author function is the tying of the text to my name. The author is
> that sum of circumstance under one name. I am one such entity.)

*
**

Then came again the cloister-wild of Sundays and suicide. I could not
name the season; the city of gold had gone grey;
I saw no needed meaning in my days.
The wings in my chest gave a heave and a flap.
I lay in my bed on my back.

Sarah had been going to pill herself.
She had even gone so far as to line her paracetamol up, like Thumbkin.
It would have taken days, she said (having googled it afterwards).
Then her cousin killed herself, took all the medication given to her to help
govern her twin and warring poles,
and Sarah knew the crazy grief which slaps at thin air

And in the darkest days when my bones throbbed with sobs and it felt like
my heart was going to lurch out and my lungs rang from remembering,
intermittently and with little conviction, to breathe,
when my sleeps were long and dreamless and when I woke I would cry
that I could no longer be asleep –

At dinner, once, with friends discussing people they had known when
young:
and what of Pete, oh what was his name? (jubilation, giggling)
oh no, no, he committed –

(My parents' faces falling)

Would I too ever be cause for mid-dinner pause?
and apparently too he was just the most cheerful guy

I watch tabloids attempt to bring the Mediterranean-borne corpses of infants into some kind of Old Testament iconography. As long as they are drowning in the Mediterranean, it's Exodus. If they're at the entrance to the Channel Tunnel, it's a plague swarm.

> For little sister
> I grow afeared
> of the time that is coming for you
> when all those you know who want to be women
> will speak of the bits of their bodies
> which they do not like,
> and of the adverts you will see
> of women laughing alone with salads.
> But I am soothed to think of the cast that will call to you,
> that I may be one of them;
> and how rich your co-construction shall be.

(self/cancellatory)

Blood orange season.
I, in the bath, was bleeding the habitual chunks the doctors brushed off even when
I told them again and again of my pain.
It hurt, so the bath was very hot.
Then out came a thing that was not usual.
The size of a lentil, and shaped like a bean,
with a loose tendril like a sprout.
It would not squish under my thumb when I tried.
Was it? I thought.
No. Could be.
Weeks later the doctor bluntly would say:

a heavy period or an early miscarriage are nearly always the same thing.
Don't think about it, move on.
She was right. I didn't really think about it
except about the fact that I was not thinking about it.
Such a self-cancellatory event. The realisation dual, and ambush.
In private you go through the motions but also, can't be bothered. I
drained the bath and ushered the little overcooked bulghur clots down;
afterwards on the road lay a crescent knotted orange and red in a skin
sack of gore,
sticky in the sun, and ignored.

In my twentieth summer,
I began boldly asking Filipina women when I saw them. This was perhaps
because they reminded me of my grandmother, with whom I amblingly
sought to make amends for years of disinterest and mutual incompatibility.
I would pin the two and twos together: the nametags would say Mercy
and the hairs on our heads would be the same-gauge wire. When I asked
them if they were Filipina they would say yes with a happy glaze entering
their eyes – this country the main export of which is people, who come to
mop cold corridors in foreign parts, or soothe us with the softness of their
accents, and send balikbayan. To which I would reply with joy me too!
A half! They always said I did not look it. Once I stumbled on *Pampanga*.

(An Interview, Imagined)

Tell me about the Philippines.

Well within the colonised it bears something quite particular
they say the Austronesians when they plied forth on their pirogues,
were grated up on to these shoals and sands
because of currents.
And similarly, in the Pacific,
we are quite hot property at this crossroads of the South China Sea (see
only: Scarborough)
so we had the Chinese too.
And before, but between, Muslim traders from Jakarta, who have given us
words in dialect such as *salamat*.
Then the Spanish, whose crown prince's name we still bear, when most
others have cast off

Have I told you of the galleons?
Greatest of their craft, and weighing one hundred thousand tons, replete
with silks and silver? The journey to Alta California took four months,
one of which alone was spent getting out from among the spined islands,
a most deadly, volcanic constellation.
And then the British, briefly, from whom America came to wrangle.

I have known people to resent I have not made it more apparent.

There are those who would read in the planes of my face what they
wanted,
the fictions they wished me to fill, or the cut-out behind which it might be
convenient to crouch.

I will braise it into dishes for your delectation.

My peers knew nothing of the Philippines. They travelled in arcs through Southeast Asia, but it was Vietnam they stopped in for street food. They took mushrooms on the beach in Thailand. The pictures trickled back: coconut-bounded cocktails with little candy-coloured paper parasols, frangipani flowers plucked and tucked behind one ear, open shirts and bintang beer, swimwear under waterfalls and endless (endless!) pictures of gleefully riding mopeds. They did not know about the first overthrow of colonial rule in Southeast Asia, or José Rizal, or that the Spanish was the first empire on which the sun never set, or the People Power revolution (as recently as 1986!) which ricocheted, reappearing elsewhere.

Tell me about José Rizal.

He was an ophthalmologist. He also discovered an eagle and two types of butterfly when in exile on Mindanao. He had terrible eyesight but was nonetheless arrestingly good-looking. He advocated for self-representation in the Cortes Generales, much like to this day what Puerto Rico does not have. A modest demand, you would think. So they shot him.

Tell me about revolution.

It was the summer of 1986. I was doing my prelims at the time. It was so exciting, because every time I came out of an exam there were updates. The coverage was very good, because it was an easy place for journalists. English-speaking, lots of sex.

At the sit-ins, the best was lunchtime. Everyone just sat down, got out packed lunches and ate together. People picked their way through the crowds with ube rice cakes wrapped in banana leaves. Even in the hot sun, sitting on a freeway overpass!

My father and I had said in unison once before: Manila light! at the
strange mercurials quickening
he smiled at me, that I had noticed.

Half-Filipina
          – well actually a quarter
what?

A fragile sense of self shattered on the Etoile roundabout.
The eternal flame at the Tomb of the Unknown Soldier has been
extinguished only once:
after the Euros in 1992 someone pissed on it.

It was a firing squad on December 30th, 1898. It is said his last words were
Consummatum Est,
but that could well be wishful thinking.

When my father's trueblood pinoy is probed the deflection has been
(by some) the word *mestizo*. An eighteenth-century system to split the
muddling of the blood by degrees and iterations:

'Spanish and Indian: *mestizo*'
'Mestizo and Spanish woman: *castizo*'
'Castizo woman and Spaniard: *Spaniard*'
'Spanish woman and Black man: *mulatto*'
'Spanish and mulatto: *morisco*'
'Morisco woman and Spaniard: *albino*'
'Spaniard and albino: *torna atrás*'
'Indio (Indian) and torno atrás: *lobo*'
'Lobo and Indian woman: *zambaigo*'
'Zambaigo and Indio woman: *cambujo*'

I went to Manila the summer I slumped into depression
a word which speaks to me as of the state of gas in a quickly closing
chamber.
The wings were unfolded now and drying in the warmth of me, and the
shadow foe beneath them rocked on its haunches on the sill of my chest.
I could not heave it out, and struggled to breathe.
But had I gone so as to use the monsoon as pathetic fallacy for my state of
mind? Or to rediscover an auto-orientalised sense of self? I rode on the
roof of a jeepney and when the fare collector climbed aboard to tell me
the rain was coming I kicked myself for noting it Conradian. Why had I
not equipped myself for this? I read the Noli. It struck me as having been
written in a hurry. Previously, in England, I had felt compelled to make
it loudly known. This performance of otherness was for their benefit,
because I felt without it they might always have this knowledge gap, and
this was not something I wished for them.
I startled myself, marking the jungle and all its truisms.
I stepped off the plane in Bacolod (an Arabic C, mind you), provincial
capital of Negros Occidental. Here I can feel you holding your breath. You
are waiting. I can feel you waiting. A hush not so much of respect but of
expectation. You are waiting for me to tell you how the air was close, that
it was hot, that the atmosphere and then fairly quickly my self, was sticky.
There was the ruptured cone of a volcano, black and bright green, and
there were thin tall palm trees like a print our father kept.

> At the height of the Spanish Empire
> it took one year for a letter to reach Madrid from Manila.
> Manila was not alone in being known as the
> pearl of the orient

Hong Kong claims the call,
and Sri Lanka, Ho Chi Minh (née Saigon), Penang and Goa.
Beware pearls.
they are often a moniker
glossing the grit
(there's the rub!)
of possession.

> (I shall stand in the room with twin fists
> holding only your name in my mouth.)

olan is rain in Ilonggo
I grated a coconut
saw a baby carabao
and a tuna riding to market in a sidecar.

Cutting an eel in the slapdash kitchen sink from a bucket where they
whorled after ditch-fishing like languishing ampersands
eased
his long bright blade in
:
red.
Marvel at my own surprise, of course!
red red red red red
big bright blade sawing now
beribboned life still moving like a woman's unbikinied legs.
I had never known so red
because their death is always so far away.
Blood is the convenience of claim.

José Rizal in towns where stucco statues made him look the groom on
every wedding cake.

Driving around the Philippines Lola liked to tell me about her family's wealth.

Her father ordered a piece of Carrara marble for a tabletop, but it got chipped in shipping.

He designed a dining room table with adjustable legs for children's parties.

His mother's house had fifty horses and hardwood floors.

She had six pregnancies! And thirty hats!

There was a shoe shop here where if you took the cloth of your party dress they could dye your pumps the exact same colour.

The doctor who delivered your father induced me because he said, If I do not deliver Caring Sy-Quia's grandson there will be hell to pay.

When we were children we knew Russian émigrés that had come down through Vladivostok years before. She brought all her furs, but they lived out their days in the cooler of a meat-packing warehouse, for the flies.

There are other uncles of history in that photo, I was told.

I considered this. Our family given special precedence at Rizal Day observances. We spring from the loins of his sister, her maiden name. How we smudge it when it suits us.

The first overthrow of colonial rule in Southeast Asia. No small thing. He was a very good-looking man.

I was sent in part to meet my grandfather. This was a man whose shoulders had been in the sides of pictures. The album of Lola's nineteenth birthday. My mother designed my dress. She had good taste. And what she said, went, you know. Oh my. It was quite an eventful party. Herein followed how much importance to accord.

He talked for a while about chasing them through Europe and running
out of money, eating hotel mints.
Breakfast at the Shangri-La. My eggs bleeding out as he glosses over.
He says they did not mention how nice you are to look at, how he'd be
mad about me if he were twenty-three.
Then he closed a wad of cash into my hand.

I sobbed a little softly for all the absences in a childhood not my own.

Then I met my father's nanny, name Pining. The one who held my father,
before the Austrian, before being taken to his mother in Spain.
I crossed the line into the kitchen
on the face of it to say Pining, it was delicious.
I think of my father standing here, last time, secret, crying, saying
goodbye to her –
she was a presence not pointed out to me then.
(Not even cropped, just never in the pictures)
She is visiting to see me but kept behind out back
making siu mai from scratch unthanked
for the hands that held him when he cried
now I know
his impulse for kind well-weathered women's faces
and I who cried
upon meeting her like all most
moments of portent
in kitchens
I think this
this all rushing in
my father

standing in monsoon Manila light.
The palms and the mangoes,
a little nipa blown away
a woman speaking a mestizo language
the breath in darkness
that we remember as the topography
of the safe place; the place which is before fear
rushing

                rushing in

this is why I came
she says this hug is for him
I can only say he misses you
I wonder what it's like having the baby you raised reclaimed
something rushed and broke we held one another tight
she grabbed me as if she knew I was only just afloat in the
monster-mere between my lungs
like she knew what state I came from
her smile is of love
and mine is like his she says
now I write at the kitchen counter where
she peels pomelo for me whole
knife-flicking
he loves mangoes just like you she says
and holds me tight

On the parvis piazza square of the Church of the Black Nazarene,
Lola taught me to choose Chinese grapefruits by weighing them with a
bounce of the hand, so as to secure the juicy ones. She told me the secret
is getting the segments out whole. She taught me a mango is sweetest
nearer the skin. She bought me strings of mangosteen which I recognised
to compare to bulbs of garlic in strands, and knots of the luminous orbs
known as lanzones. She showed me the taste of the tiny lime known as
calamansi, the juice of which can be served hot or cold.

She showed me how to cook steak, oxtail stew, poke fish; bought me
an œillet-patterned balconet bra. Her hands are fine-boned like birds,
her nails long and neat and sanded into smooth crescents. She showed
me churches built from big blocks of coral which sit at the edges of the
windowwash-coloured sea, identical in face to those which pepper
Mexican hills, miles and miles away.

In London pomelos are hard to find. The first time I saw one I jumped for
joy.
Someday soon, the one I love will bring me a pomelo from a stall along
Whitechapel Road, and my first thought will be that this is the moment
in the formula wherein a chosen person comes bearing the secret, potent,
magical, all-unlocking thing.

Pining tells me something no one else would have:
how when Lola came back to claim him
Pining was sent into the provinces with my toddler father
to hide.
And in the night
somebody came
and snatched him by his ankles from the bed:
Lola, twenty-five and furious
and how we cried, me and ma'am Caring, when she took him away from us.
But enough now, I cry.
She is polishing the silver, with curls of newspaper.
The twilight came so fast like Kodachrome.

The typhoon flipped the banana leaves inside out and I found myself thinking
of my father in our new house in Paris,
lying in a camp bed (having scarce furniture) one Sunday morning to torrential rain
saying softly
it reminds me of Manila
of course our mother was the only one to catch his meaning then but
standing in the rains remembered by my father I recalled
him with his children gathered close in little duvet-scoops,

> (he adores his children the way a woman does,
> in this way he is unlike them all
> my mother has told me twice.)

and him remembering the rains
in Manila.

In the photos was a fifth: the great-uncle who died of AIDS. And right before, in the London hospital where the certificate was issued reading only *leukaemia*, he started speaking Spanish, so no one could record the contours of his final saying.

I am told I would have loved him very much.

In the harbour of Barcelona, Christopher Columbus's statue (Isabella sold some pearls to pay – Lola impressing this upon me in a black and yellow taxi) pointing.
In Portugal they were so angered at Magellan that they chiselled off his coat of arms
and so it is unknown!
Lapu Lapu holding silvered spear in Cebu City intersection
clubbed him to death. Famous circumnavigator. It was a battle on a beach.

And in your shadow language
the meanings that crouch inside the words you gave me
wrapped in the old cocoons of things palmed to you in your turn of time,
and my father knew all this. He knew each and every thing.
I needed to unwrap them and see myself the cracks.
And he did know of the shadow-foe, but it was not for him to save me.

Women made my father:
gritty women with grey in their hair,
women who swear,
women with tough patches on their hands from holding
(my mother has callouses on her hands from all the steadfasting she has
assumed)
women who impress things on me in black and yellow taxis
women who fall off bicycles clumsily
women bound and unbound by blood

I have clung to this as if indeed I were drowning.
All through the grey English days.

The shadow-foe lives in Sundays. It will come for you and suggest all the
most horrible things. It will come gliding with the slither that makes no
noise, surprise you, align with your spine. It will seep into the marrow of
you. On days like this, tell it to do away with subterfuge.
Welcome that which has been sadly peeking in
and all others who would seek to come in from the cold.
Sit and eat.

(It is only a visitor, and it is the code of the road
                                       to leave no one out in the cold.
                                                          Then fling it
                       from the window. See it unfold from its wings,
                                   flap and fly away, soar, diminish.)

In the Scottish Borders in the week leading up to it,
we ate brie paninis with cranberry jam.
At Lindisfarne, Ben wore an anorak which billowed in keeping with his
statements on the feelings of history.

The sea was slatey, clean, and cold.
You could look across it (as I did) and think of Vikings bringing us the
bones
of our most brutal language.
Many raids' worth of axe wounds.
The gospels going wrapped in blankets.
The hills purpled with flowers.

We crested the hill with Hadrian's trace, just as
our prime minister spoke of himself in the present perfect.
Our knuckles were all in our mouths.
*I am very proud and very honoured to have been Prime Minister of this
country*

                         WE DID NOT NEED EUROPE AT DUNKIRK!
                              (that boat Tamzine that lies on the floor)

Years and years from now, when this has settled like sediment in a glass,
I should like to think we will remember
The persistence with which we were all humiliated.

(This is where I leave you:
crossing the borders back)

You might think this is the ending sought all this time: a rupture of the world believed to be known. It is the event that is demanded in Classical narratology.

But this is not Classical narratology.

My sentences, with their linearity, have duped you.

I am disrupting the categorising impulse.

My longings are slippery like fish.

I am eluding your impulse.

I am trying my best.

A poetics for speaking to the drift

And it broke Nana's heart. When first she began to die,
the sound in her ears was like whale song
and she took on the glazed gaze of one pearl diver, who washed up
on the sofa

> (prior the pressure had kept her contained,
> it was this drift she had feared.)

her gnarled knuckles like the roots of a tree, or a mooring
(for me)
her mind became a seashell,
an enconched roster of arguments,
shoring them up against the century she'd lived and breathed.
The dust in Warsaw five years after.
The crumpets with no butter. A very sad thing.
All her nights of homework, blared open by air raid sirens.
Her cousin killed by submarine.
The Russian army entitled to rape every woman they found. Her friend,
seventeen and sleeping in the last days before the fall of Berlin. Woken
by a soldier flicking off the covers over her, and his officer saying это
слишком мало (that one is too little).
So they went off to rape her mother.
The Six Day War. Stockpiling fruit juice so the baby could survive.

> – I had not met anyone with whom I was prepared to have a child.

How unlike the climate of the time, that she did not bow.
Nana's daughter was not raised to understand that Germany had been one
place.
What had been the duty?
Twenty-eight years after the fall of the Third Reich
her husband having fought
her homework having been bombed.

They moved to (West) Germany.
They believed in Europe greatly.
They had only one child.
But this daughter was raised in the sincere belief that there was something greater than nations;
so when the prime minister of this my dying island began to speak of himself in the present perfect

                         (what is this place's penchant for boat metaphors?)
that was when my grandmother began to joke about wanting to die.

In Berlin, my mother's tears are rolling to meet the field of incongruous rye.
       – It didn't come out of nowhere, you know.
All that summer, the news was full
of people riding the trains through Hungary to Austria and freedom,
hanging on to the sides of them,
with their *children*.

Now we come to November of that year.
The morning of, I woke to check facts and spot rogue commas. I howled in the foremorning for all the futures being foreclosed.
Kristallnacht, the falling of the Wall (the early days after of which, green-grocer windows were smashed, for their bananas), and also the flight of Kaiser Wilhelm.
The imperial order was falling, and what replaced it?
When we talk about the end, we talk about the *c o l l a p s e* of the USSR.
It failed, so we won. Us and our Levi's 501s.

       – I am telling you! It is a cursed day.

                     (My mother, down the phone)
I am in London, weeping.
Later on I look up other things to curse the date:
in 1620 on this day, the *Mayflower* first spotted land.

I did some of the driving.
I did it out of a sense of social justice.
He never dared touch her.
That one is too little.
He beat her.
He beat him.
Admitto te.
Consummatum est.
I vow.

   – You know, a lot of what we think we know about Jesus has
been disproved by the Nag Hammadi texts.
 How they were found: in the ploughing of an Egyptian field, a tall earthen
jar was found. When its seal was broken the first thing to emerge on the
invitation of the breeze was papyrus flakes.
   – It was just some peasant who found them

                            (Nana uses the word peasant)
The jar was carried home and its contents used to light fire.
On these pieces of papyrus, it is written that Jesus bedded Mary Mag,
and liked it too.
   – The whole thing was sort of covered up.
She is reaching for soup at ninety-one
and I am startled by the beauty of her hands, those knuckles that a ring
could not slide over.
She is the woman who believes in the harm done by mistranslation.
She shielded her baby from the sun with her hands.
She seduced a priest. She cut up her coat to make a teddy bear.

Her notebook. Dated 1957. Black like papal lace. Notes on the Gospels of
St Mark.
A folded flyleaf secret fell.
Splayed its cream ribs on the floor.
My grandfather's handwriting. His Ds so beautiful.
Do not let her know you have seen that!

Says my mother, askancing over.
I curled my toes over the edge of knowing,
but it was too big.

In Manila came news that Paul, who was my namesake's husband, had
died. *Er war mein richtiger Vater*, said my father to my mother.
Paul, who called me *chérie* and later, *ma grande*.

And one year later to the day, I woke in tears after a dream where he had
appeared a young ghost, be-jumpered in green with black-framed glasses,
a blond swath making him generic of his age, and told me with a flash of
mid-century grin, *oui chérie, tout va bien*. I was in their hallway. Their
smell of cigarettes, chintz, and white port.

All the above: the particulars which crowd up and inform,
which I cannot sweep aside.
If you whittle them away you leave me bereft, reduced, inaccurate, and
squared.
Let us by all means be specific, but if that means that in your ruling I am
of this shallow valed country, then we cannot ignore my grandmothers,
steely-nerved across the moor, the bare ground they crossed, rising in
some distant corridor to specify *Castellano*, or learning to speak German.
My insubordinate legiances spill over, seep. Watch me weep.

I have wandered through the rivers of the night
seeking he who would willingly receive
the love I longed to divest.

But did they deceive
in leading me to believe
that such a thing would make me whole?

Where would you have me bleed for you?

It was 'Air and Angels'!
So thy love may be my love's sphere;

It is the high summer, and the wildfires are always getting worse. I cannot
seem to bring my heartbeat back from the edge, it is always quietly
climbing up to break-breast speeds. Until all of a sudden I am in
so much pain I cannot breathe.

The magazines scream that the world is burning. Which it is.
And I am aching that it would be unethical to have a child here,
to sentence someone to life.

My mother taught me
you do not in fact need men to carry
heavy boxes for you.
Instead, you can decline their offers of assistance
and in so doing impress them in a way they were not expecting.
(This will give you a competitive advantage.)

All the most seminal poets are dying.
There was one who lived on an island and
planted trees all the
long days of his life.
He wrote a poem about a forest
what was that poem
it had a line about the forgotten
what was that poem, it had me
hook line and sinker
once.

There is no end. The doors of revelation and arrival will always swing croaking on their hinges if you see their crossing as the place.

You shall know those you have been called upon to love by the way they say your name,
for it will sound safe in their mouth.

You will make excellent love in all that you do.

These were the things said only once.

When writing on the body of the beloved, it is common to compare it to
new lands, as if one were exploring, setting
footfall in unshallowed shoals
replete with unknown beasts.
We have a cult of progress,
euphemisms of contact,
a fallacy of arrival.
I have travelled to this meeting place,
I am meeting you in this trammelled space –

Epilogue: Epithalamion

(a song to cover the cries of a bride; the commemoration of a definitive marriage; to be at the threshold)

I know how to cook rice, now.
I have eaten cakes whose names
sound like hope
and seen strings of pearls like
disappointment
hung in
the market that smelled of grease.

> (We went to Rome, and I looked for my grandfather
> in the frank incensed half-dark, wearing my reverence
> as a church-appropriate sundress, but he was not there.)

Lola writes:

We did not run away to Munich, but to Hamburg.

>   (At that time, my mother's first cousin was the Philippine
>   General Consul in that city and she lived in a villa.)

Whilst in Hamburg, I went to dinner at the home of another relative, whose husband had the post as the representative of the Philippine National Bank.

>   (He had gotten this post through my mother's intervention.)

The dinner was in honour of a German who was on his way to a posting in the Philippines. Luck would have it that said German then bumped into your father's father at the first cocktail party he was invited to. German then mentioned he had met me at a dinner party in Hamburg. How my mother found out that your grandfather had left Manila for Hamburg to try and find us is something, now half a century hence, I do not know. Anyway Kia phoned her cousin the General Consul and she packed us off

>   in her official Mercedes with her driver.

Nana says (on the phone, her voice shaking, shuffling through the sheaf I
sent her, first class post)

And then we get to here, where you write they must have fucked/because
he was defrocked. We did not, in fact, as you have it, *fuck* until we got
married. And I did not seduce him! He thought about it very seriously.

Yes but Nana I do not necessarily mean you persuaded him into bed with
you, I mean you were a woman who knew words in Old Hebrew and the
Gospel of Matthew

Yes I see. Well with regards to the fruit juice when we were in Libya.

We got in touch with two other families, a French one and an English
one to go in convoy. If we'd gotten separated it would have been very bad.
There was a war on. It was a very bad moment, I must say.

Yes yes it's true,

She was the length of my hands

To sort out his damnation that's a bit hard. I know I'm opposed to the
Catholic Church but it was very important to him.

Then you say at the end they did not love each other. It's true we had some
difficulties. You can keep that in but if you get to be as old as I am you get
to be quite careful about saying whether or not people love each other.

                             It's quite stark, saying we did not

      love each other.

And the people who found the Nag Hammadi texts were looking for bird
shit for fertiliser, not ploughing a field.

And you know I am not *the* woman who believes in the harm done by
mistranslations, there are many of us.

His Ds so beautiful – it's true, they were.

I AM WRITING NOW from the inky heart of empire,
its assonance no more unknown to me.
I shall knock the pillars out from under you
and label you up
in room upon room
of Wedgwood blue.

I HAVE SHUFFLED ALL THE SHARDS of what came to me broken
and I have not pried, for dealing in shards is what I wanted;
these being my inheritance.

THESE BEING
my demands
my thanks
my by rights

I USED TO WORRY that the performance was never quite for my own
benefit;
that I owed it to others, that without me they might never apprehend and
therefore I was duty-bound to make the point
again and again,
with the quiet militancy of washing rice before cooking it in a saucepan.
This had been the extent of it: cooking rice.
But it is possible, as I have found, to delineate blood-bearings to each
their own.
My brother, for instance, is less interested in this quandary.
My father, for instance, professes to be half, which would make me a
quarter.
I reserve his right to do so; but my claim is my own.

> (And when it comes to the men of my family,
> I do not think it has nothing to do with
> their command of desire, depending.)

Who was Emaré?
One who was given a coat embroidered with love stories
so that when donned
she was clothed in romance.

She fled.
She wandered.
The coat weighed.
Until she cast it off.
And then,
she was free.
Her shoulders bare
with their allusive curves.

All the uses of my body and what others would have me put it to.
Blood is so contrived.
Texts are porous.
I am walking
from one
to the other.
I am clothed in romance.
I am casting it off.

Like this I am primeval as a woman in a sundress.
I have become one of the gritty women, with freckles peppering the loose
skin of their arms.
I am walking through a many-furrowed field
which in relinquished seasons is feathered with asparagus.
In this late light of an early century, the ash shades of earth and stubble,
I plight (give, pledge) you my troth (fealty, loyalty, truth).

Palazzo della Signoria – the ceiling with Penelope and other female
virtues (on business with my mother. In the evenings, mozzarella that
oozed with the pleasure of being eaten). Even then, I had inklings: when I
looked at the female virtues on the ceiling.

> (The position I would need to be in to contemplate
> Esther sitting strong in her faith.)

And when the stories are shrugged from my shoulders, then I am free.
You are the bedrock of all that I am.
All the days of my life
shall be to honour you
in every thing I do.
Now I walk.

A marriage should not be a forsaking of all others. It is instead a many-
witnessed act. I stand before you today (I imagine myself saying) with the
emotional health to choose this person because of all of you. I can face the
enormity of this decision because of you. I know what love is because of
you: its bluntness, its grittiness.

I am here, the bottom bracket of a most-loathed generation.
All the joys promised to me. And those potencies playing out in other
theatres of war,
our little civilian lives of hitherto peace
the future endless no more,
violence, like money, stored offshore.
Your coming over the threshold was marked.
My equivalent days were opposed.
It was stark.
When we came over the hill with our knuckles all in our mouths,
it was something I'd seen:
a hit-and-run future which had come for us like the slice of a knife.
And the world we knew was all wrong: too hot, and unjust.

Nonetheless, your coming was heralded with the triumphs of the civilian over regime.

Let us enter into oaths knowingly. So I ask you now in the presence of this company.

> ('And of course,' volunteered my father
> to my friend, 'my best friend, I married.')

In defiance of state.

It is the vowing which interests me.
I call upon these persons here present.
The cause for which marriage was ordained (this is not included in the civil script, having been cut in twain at the time of the burnings)
to love and to cherish
from this day forward
incumbent on me
all that I am I give to you.

> (but were they their all, at the time of
> their giving? And how did they know?)

(I am suspicious of this knowledge which apparently simply descends.)
Then they shall give their troth to each other.

> (the deep bone know)

from this day forward
put asunder
against all manner of foes.
Have you never been held by all the limbs of a woman?

Callum and I eat a cheese. We walk for hours and look at art.
Arthur makes a single Yorkshire pudding which looks like Anatolia.
I am making little waves with my carrot, as if it were a cigarette.

There are long conversations: in bars, in kitchens, in the illegal extensions of council house flats. We get drunk too much. We know nothing about wine. We spend our money on shoes. We press our palms together to dance in the amber-coloured oak-panelled dark. We bowl forth to a city that didn't really want us.

Would I live forever in this country?
The thought made my throat close in.
Its chalky mid-hues. Fields like paint sample cards with whimsical names.
I will love you all my life.

When my mother vowed in the face of those persons then present
to commit to my father to the exclusion of all others,
that cold day in October with the Assyrian lions
and the red buses streaking by,
the imminent grapes,
my mother was protecting my father from the violence which could come
for him
in the night or the day, at work or at rest,
and take him back to the islands where little love waited for him.
My mother was twenty-one, bullish and
knew nothing.
It was her boldest act in the time of walls falling.

All over the world.
My father resents this narrative.
He says it was love.
Which it was.
But we must not forget
the bodies that eyed this union for a full year after.
My parents are brave
and the choices I make will be made
in the vault of this precedent.

They made us a world where private, witnessed love could win over nations and all the stories they told.
They made me richer, for all these confusions.
My parents made a promise in the face of the state. They stared it down. When asked all the monumental questions they replied: I do.
Between them and those present.

But my parents also did something which was within the most primal framework of the state.
I propose something different.
A love so unsanctioned, no promises exist for it.

Hitherto, society has been underpinned by the institution of marriage. The covenant. The sacrament. It has been used for the warehousing, at its most recent and benign, of intelligent women.
I call for a reordering of its ceremonies. I call upon those persons here present today. I solemnly swear. I pledge to relinquish the matrimonial retreat which has ordered us unto this brink.
As we hurtle towards the coughing future, I promise to hold tight to you.
I promise to hold you up and hold you close and hold you down when you feel you may go spinning off the earth.
All that I am I share with you.
I promise my presence in good times and bad. In suchness, and even in the eventuality of wealth.
I wish you good fortune in the time that we will travel through together, and the changes
that we will forgive in ourselves and in others.
I promise to stand by your side as we move through changing worlds.
I promise to respect you, and query you when I am in doubt.

I made my friend smile. One of his best smiles, the ones that knock the
knees out from under the sun.
I had made him a birthday banner.
He saw it coming up the garden path.
I was in the dining room.
He smiled up at me.
It tackled me sideways, this smile burning into my memory,
tackling all my pre-empts by surprise.
My beautiful beaming friend.
I made him smile.
It was the most beautiful thing I'd ever seen.
It tackled me sideways.
Him smiling on the garden path, turning twenty-three.
That flush of love.
My friends whom I adore.
It stuns me how it runs so deep.
I am amazed. How? Where the warning?
This friendship form to take.
It sloshes in the cup.
I swore no solemn oaths.
And yet in these times when I brim and spill with grief
at the time's consequence,
I find myself at the foot of this most sacred undertaking:
to love and defend in the present tense; with no deferral or commingling;
to be my lone line self and look the monumental questions in the eye;
to defend you all until my lungs give out.

You have made me gentle,
you have made me brave.
In these the weeks of our need,
we have come to one another
on the tides of work and day.
We are charging at the best befores of our rage,
a most minimum thing this age commands.

I will defend you all until my lungs give out.
I will love you all my life.

All these things being said, it is not always necessary to operate only
at the register of vow;
you may suffice yourself with subtext
and all its crowds.

And the bitten truth is this:
when I am with you, teleology drops away,
and the days need have no given meaning.
For, in the quiet of your company,
I am of consolate closeness
and bristle of it along every pore.
And standing by your sides,
I feel steadied and prepared
to face the yawn of years.

Acknowledgements

Thank you to my agent, Matthew Marland, for taking on this strange beast of a book. Thank you to Rachael Allen, co-creative editor of dreams. Thank you to Hamish Ironside, Christine Lo, David Pearson and Phoebe Barker, and everyone at Granta, for giving this text a place to land and so much care. I am so grateful to all of you.

Thank you to my friends who read the book at various stages – Ellen Slatkin, Suzie Marshall (who did so twice!), Will Forrester, Hamish Forbes and Ella Bucknall. Enormous thanks to Sarah Howe for her attention and encouragement, and to all the Ledbury Critics and mentors, in particular Sandeep Parmar. Thanks to Houman Barekat and Rowan Borchers for answering all of my questions, and for the sheer pleasure of their company.

It took me nine years to write this book, and almost as long to take it, and myself, seriously. Thanks are due to the staff of Shakespeare and Company in Paris, and the people I met there, for offering an environment in which I, and so many others, might begin to imagine ourselves as writers. In a similar vein, thank you to Kiran Millwood Hargrave, whose praise after my first ever open mic in 2014 proved vital. I have also been incredibly lucky, over the course of my education, to have had many great teachers in humanities subjects. Special mentions go to Rob Grady, Charlotte Cornell, Matt Gardner, David Felton, Dr Elizabeth Pidoux, Prof. James Soderholm and, though she may have found it deeply awkward at the time, my mother, who put me on to John Donne. At university, special thanks go to Prof. Michael Whitworth, Dr Aisling Byrne and Prof. Richard McCabe, who put me on to George Herbert; and Dr Michelle Kelly, who firmed up my thinking on anecdotes and fractured histories.

The last year of this book's formation was the most intense: I went freelance and was absolutely terrified. My housemates at the time – the aforementioned Suzie, Charlie Atkins, and Monica Gupta – were unwaveringly supportive, as were Harry Bush and Alannah Jones. Thanks also to Charlie's parents, Ralph and Fiona, for the loan of their kitchen table, upon which much of the final writing took place. Thank you to Tom Bloom and Juliette Tuke for giving me a job when I really needed one – and for making it such a pleasure. Thank you to Lucasta Miller, Ian Bostridge, and their children, Oliver and Ottilie, for welcoming me into their home when I moved to London (and before them, to the Hallsted-Baumerts: Sheila, Eric, Alizée and William).

Thank you, once again, to my family, for giving me their blessing to pursue this work. Thank you to the constellation of chosen family I have inherited: Fiona Stewart; Andrew McCulloch; Suzie Ivelich; Jack Loh; Margaret Simpson, Douglas Booth, and their children; Stephanie Molère and her late husband Paul; Marina Roosevelt and her late husband Curtis; and to that which I've chosen myself: not yet mentioned are Juliana Bergen and, of course, T. Thank you all for teaching me everything I know about joy.

The epigraph in English is taken from 'The Thunder, Perfect Mind' from the Nag Hammadi library, translated by George W. MacRae. The epigraph in Coptic is taken from 'The Thunder: Perfect Mind', in *The Coptic Gnostic Library – A Complete Edition of the Nag Hammadi Codices*, ed. James M. Robinson, *The Nag Hammadi Studies* volume XI (1979).

Lines from 'The Flea' by John Donne are reproduced on page 47.

The line 'Rest your human head, my love' on page 48 is inspired by a line from 'Lullaby' by W. H. Auden.

Lines from 'Erlkönig' by Johann Wolfgang von Goethe are reproduced on pages 56 and 57.